THE ONE SONG

All Is One

Jeannie Carrera *Chow Yoke Lin*

PARTRIDGE
A Penguin Random House Company

To order additional copies of this book, contact
Toll Free 800 101 2657 (Singapore)
Toll Free 1 800 81 7340 (Malaysia)
orders.singapore@partridgepublishing.com

www.partridgepublishing.com/singapore

CONTENTS

Foreword vii

Chapter one: We Come From Paradise 1

Chapter two: All Are Little Bennies 4

Chapter three: Mrs. Saw's Visitor 7

Chapter four: Henry's Answer 11

Chapter five: In Search Of Self 13

Chapter six: Corridor Of Mirrors 19

Chapter seven: Koonii And His Mistakes 23

Chapter eight: Kenneth's Activities 28

Chapter nine: Edward's Journey 31

Chapter ten: Henry's Promise 36

Chapter eleven: I Am Home Again 45

Chapter twelve: Koonii's Sacrifice 51

Chapter thirteen: The Enemy Is Us 56

Chapter fourteen: The Mirror 63

Chapter fifteen: Ye Are A Part Of Me 69

Chapter sixteen: The Culmination 73

Chapter seventeen: The Eternal Moment 80

Chapter eighteen: All Is One 87

FOREWORD

For all who wish to find the JOY in the hearts, FAIRNESS in the minds and the LOVE in the soul. See LOVE in everything, in times of joy and in times of sadness, see the positive side of everything and you will experience the TRUTH. LOVE is all there is. All is LOVE. There is nothing but LOVE.

If you see LOVE in everything, you experience LOVE. Only LOVE.

JEANNIE CARRERA CHOW YOKE LIN

CHAPTER ONE

We Come From Paradise

Tirips Mlaer is a paradise. No, in fact it is a shangri-la. All the inhabitants live in close knitted communities. They sing from dawn till dusk. Laughter is heard in every corner. There is enough food for everyone and nobody grows old.

Elos is sixteen years old. He has many brothers and sisters. He loves dancing and singing with them. They play many games together. However, Elos feels something missing in their lives. Every day, they just sing and dance and enjoy themselves. There is nothing else to do.

One day, Elos is sitting alone by himself beside the lovely lake. He is deep in thought, "What if there is something else to do besides singing, dancing and enjoying life?"

"What do you wish to do, little one?" a voice asks.

Elos startles and turns to see the elderly, wise woman of the paradise standing behind him.

"I wish for some different activities to do," Elos answers as he pouts his lips, "I wish I can experience something other than singing, dancing and enjoying myself every day."

"What exactly do you wish to experience?" the wise woman asks.

Elos ponders and wonders out loud, "What if other than singing, dancing and enjoying there are also other opposite activities that I can experience every day?"

"Do you really wish to experience the opposite activities as well?" the wise woman looks deeply into Elos' eyes.

"Yes, yes, that would be a change from this boring life. We just eat and enjoy ourselves here. Is there a place where we can experience something different?" Elos wonders again.

"We can think of something. We need some volunteers to experience the additional opposite activities with you. Now, who would like to share new and different experiences with Elos?" the wise woman announces to the other inhabitants who have gathered around the lake.

"I volunteer, I wish to help you to experience the additional opposite activities," Frisco, Elos's friend exclaims holding up her hands.

Elos claps his hands in glee, "You do, do you, you will help me to experience all the additional opposite activities?" Elos jumps around excitedly. "Thank you, thank you, oh, thank you so much!"

"In order to experience all the additional opposite activities, you must leave Tirips Mlaer. It is impossible to experience anything except happiness here. We will have to create another place for you. Let me see, you can go to Earth. Yes, you can experience all the additional opposite activities there," the wise woman smiles.

"I wish to go, too!" "I wish to go, too!" "I wish to go, too!" "I wish to go, too!" Many other hands fly up.

"Alright, alright, all who wish to go, may go. But, remember, when on Earth, when you experience all the additional opposite activities, REMEMBER that it is just your creation, it is not real, REMEMBER it is just an illusion" the wise woman admonishes.

"Yes, yes, we will always remember, ALWAYS!" Elos, Frisco and all the other volunteers answer cheerfully.

* * *

And so, earthlings, have you remembered that you are just here to experience all the additional opposite activities just because you found paradise too boring?

3

CHAPTER TWO

All Are Little Bennies

Little Benny is tired after a long day. He has fallen asleep under a tree. He is dreaming . . .

*   *   *

There is a lush field of beautiful flowers. They are taller than little Benny. He is enjoying the flowers. They smell nice. They are so colourful. They are so refreshing. But there is no end to the flowers. There is no way out of this floral world.

Fear suddenly grips little Benny's heart.

"Mummy! Mummy!" little Benny screams. "Where are you? I am scared!"

He is running round and round in this beautiful yet endless sea of flowers. Then, he sees a silhouette, which looks like his mother. Without a second thought, he runs excitedly towards it. He reaches the figure in no time. He grabs one of the legs, the figure turns around and little Benny sees his own face!

"Oh, I am Mummy and Mummy is me," little Benny exclaims.

"Yes, little Benny, we are one, we have always been one, we are never separated, we are always together. Don't be afraid, little one, wherever you are, there I shall be and wherever I am, there you are. Love is all there is," Mummy explains.

As his mother explains this to little Benny, more figures appear in the sea of flowers, his father, his uncles and aunts, his neighbours, his classmates, his brothers and sisters and many other strangers. All of them have little Benny's face!

Little Benny is in a world of little Bennies in a sea of beautiful flowers. He feels so serene and blessed in such a peaceful world. All is one and the same.

* * *

Little Benny wakes up from his dream. He finds himself in his mother's arms.

"Mummy, I had a dream. In the dream, you were me and I was you and I was everybody and everybody was me," little Benny says.

"I had a dream, too, little Benny. In the dream, you were me and I was you and I was everybody and everybody was me, too," his mother replies.

"That's the most wonderful experience I ever had, Remember this all your life, little Benny and treat all others as yourself and there shall be peace in the world," his mother says as she clasps little Benny's hands in hers.

CHAPTER THREE

Mrs. Saw's Visitor

It has been a gloomy day. Every day seems the same, dreary and overcast skies. They seem as grey as Mrs. Saw's face. She has been sitting before the window day after day. Her sons and daughters have all grown up. She has been looking forward to their visits since Mr Saw passed away three years ago.

The telephone never rings. The door bell never rings either. There is no laughter in the front yard. There is no shouting and screaming in the back yard either. Once upon a time, this was a noisy place, children running everywhere, laughter in the air and lots of activities going on. All these stop since the youngest boy, Sam left home five years ago. Things worsened after Mr. Saw left.

A tear rolled down Mrs. Saw's cheek. She knows all the passers-by, she waves at them whenever they passed her house. She counts them all and she knows when they will pass by her house. She knows the number of cars that will pass by her house, too.

Today, a yellow car stops in front of her house. An elderly woman struggles to get out of the driver's seat. She stands for a long time, holding the opened front door. She bends into the car to retrieve a walking stick. Slowly, she walks into Mrs. Saw's front yard. There are some beautiful roses growing along the fence. The roses seem to grow smaller and smaller each year. Mrs. Saw has neglected them.

The lady stoops to admire and smell the roses. Mrs. Saw gets up from her usual place and goes out to greet her unexpected visitor. They shake hands. The lady is Miss Cornelia, a spinster from out of town. She has been travelling to many places especially small outskirts like Mrs. Saw's neighbourhood. Miss Cornelia loves the small places. They are more cosy and friendly, she says.

"These are beautiful roses, need some care and attention, though," Miss Cornelia smiles as she looks enquiringly at Mrs. Saw.

"Yes, I have neglected them for a long time, I'm so sorry I haven't looked at them closely for so long. In fact, I've forgotten about them," Mrs. Saw replies despondently.

"Are you expecting somebody?" Miss Cornelia probes.

"No, ... Yes, ..., actually, no, uh, I've been expecting somebody for so long, it has become a habit. Every morning, I just sit at the window expecting somebody to drop by, to visit, whatever. I don't know," Mrs. Saw is confused.

"Why don't we dig this soil a bit? I think it will make the roses happy," Miss Cornelia kneels down and begins digging with a small stick.

"Yes, yes, why not?" Mrs. Saw agrees readily and follows suit.

Some moments later, both women stand up and massage their backs. They happen to look at each other and start laughing. They are a comical sight. Two old ladies trying to bend backwards rubbing their sore backs.

"Why don't you come in and have a cup of tea and some cakes?" Mrs. Saw invites Miss Cornelia into her house. Both walk gratefully into Mrs. Saw's cosy house.

"You are so lucky. Your house is so comfortable and nice," Miss Cornelia looks around as she tucks into some home baked cakes.

"It is a lonely place, all my children are away. They never visit, they never even call. They are too busy and I dare not disturb them," Mrs. Saw laments.

"Bless your children. They have a life to live. You have a life to live as well. The happiest life is a life that needs no others. An even happier life is one that ensures nobody needs you. Set them free and set yourself free, too. By giving freedom to others, you are granting freedom to yourself," Miss Cornelia observes wisely.

"Yes, I have been miserable for years because I have been relying on others to give me happiness. I cannot let go. That's why my children stay away because I am too clingy. Whenever they visit, I cannot let them leave. They are sadder than ever when it is time to leave. They stop visiting because they cannot bear the parting," Mrs. Saw suddenly sees the light.

"I understand, I have been to many places. I have seen a lot of people. The happiest people I have seen are those who search for inner happiness. The most depressed ones are those who banked on others to provide them happiness," Miss Cornelia agrees.

"Yes, yes, now I understand. Tomorrow, I will tend to my garden. I will not be sad anymore," Mrs. Saw stands up confidently as Miss Cornelia prepares to leave.

Miss Cornelia and Mrs. Saw shake hands again as they walk down the path towards the yellow car. Mrs. Saw waves until the car is out of sight. She stands there smiling for the first time in many years. Many passers-by smile back at her.

The sun is shining again in Mrs. Saw's life.

CHAPTER FOUR

Henry's Answer

Henry has killed somebody in a pub brawl. He doesn't know the person. Henry is sentenced to life imprisonment. He repents while in prison. He prays daily to God.

"Oh, God, please don't send me to hell! I didn't mean to kill him! It was self-defence. He was holding a broken wine bottle. If I didn't kill him, he would have killed me!" Henry prays day and night kneeling in his lone cell.

One day, God answers him, "Don't worry, my beloved son, you will not go to hell. If your son did something wrong, would you send him to burn in the everlasting fire?"

"But . . . but, I killed somebody. They said that killing is a crime and I will go to hell;" Henry is surprised by God's answer.

"Who are `they'," God asks Henry.

"The priests, the victim's family, the police, the law, the government . . . ," Henry mutters miserably.

"I am God, is my word less than theirs?" God queries.

"They said I deserved it. Hell is the only place suitable for criminals like me," Henry protests.

"They have made a human of God, revengeful and seeking justice and condemnation like them. God is all-powerful, all-loving, all-compassionate and all-forgiving. What does it serve God to send you to burn in an everlasting fire?" God asks gently.

"Even though I didn't mean to kill him but I have committed a crime and they said I deserved hell," Henry is flabbergasted.

"If your son killed somebody, would you burn him in an everlasting fire?" God asks Henry again.

"No, I'll forgive my son. However many times he has done wrong, I'll forgive him," Henry replies compassionately.

"So, is God less forgiving and less compassionate than you?" God asks lovingly.

". . . ." Henry is stunned and he proceeds to thank and bless God incessantly.

CHAPTER FIVE

In Search Of Self

Graem Tan is puffing hard. He is almost unconscious. He has been climbing for the past 10 days, or is it 11 days? He is not sure. This has been the toughest mountain that he has ever climbed.

Graem Tan is a most unusual person. He is never satisfied with life. He believes there is a God but where is He? He has been to as many religious buildings and climbed as many mountains in search for God. So far, he has not been successful. Where is God? God, where are you? Graem Tan is still searching.

This is his umpteenth search. He is not going to give up. But he is exhausted, his food and water supplies are running out. He must not give up. He is only 52 years old. He will not give up till he sees God with his own eyes. His eyes are closing. He cannot keep them open anymore. God, God, do not forsake me. Please do not forsake me.

"Hey, man, hey, man. You are awake," a childish voice is ringing in his ears.

Graem Tan opens his heavy eyelids. He closes them again. With much effort, he opens them again. An image is coming into view. A small face. A small, dark face. Some white teeth. Two huge dark eyes. An appealing smile. It is the face of a little boy. He is putting a water container towards Graem Tan's lips, coaxing him to drink. Then, he pours some water into a green triangular cup and tries to pour the water into Graem Tan's opened mouth.

"Where am I?" Graem Tan manages to ask after a few sips.

"I found you two days ago. You were unconscious. I pulled you onto this carpet of grass and have been waiting for you to wake up," Soona answers, beaming at Graem Tan.

"You have been here accompanying me for the past two days?" Graem Tan asks disbelievingly, staring at Soona.

"Yes, I am Soona. I live around here. I have seen many men and women come this way before. They always come in groups. You are the first to come alone. You were unconscious, so I stayed here till you are awake," Soona flashes another wide smile.

"Thank you, I am Graem Tan. I always travel alone. If not for you, I might have been eaten by some animals," Graem Tan grimaces at the prospect.

"Where are your folks?" Graem Tan wonders after he has recovered from his initial shock.

"My parents are dead. I don't know anybody else. I stay here alone by myself," Soona flashes another enchanting smile.

"Why are you here?" Soona looks inquisitively at Graem Tan.

"I am searching for something," Graem Tan answers slowly after pondering for some time. He wonders whether Soona knows about God.

"What are you searching for?" Soona persists.

"Something," Graem Tan answers simply.

"Maybe I can help you, I know this place very well. I am born here," Soona offers.

"You cannot help me to find what I am looking for," Graem Tan sighs and sits up slowly. Soona moves forward to help him up.

"Try me," Soona offers again.

"You know, I am looking for something or is it someone that doesn't exist. I suppose not in this world. I've searched in so many places. I've been to many mountains. I'm still searching," Graem Tan frowns and sighs again.

"Something or someone? You mean you are not sure what you are seeking?" Soona is perplexed.

"Oh, this is a bit difficult for you. Alright, let me tell you. I am actually searching for God. God, you know? Do you know God?" Graem Tan looks fully into the small, innocent face.

"Yes, I know God. I see God every day," Soona replies enthusiastically.

"Are you sure?" Graem Tan counters, doubtfully.

"You are searching for something that is with you every day. No wonder you cannot find it. You don't know what you are searching for," Soona seems very wise all of a sudden that Graem Tan blinks.

"What do you mean?" Graem Tan reacts defensively.

"If you are searching for God, then search no more," Soona seems to have suddenly grown very old.

"What exactly do you mean?" Graem Tan is getting furious.

"Look around you. Look at me. Feel the breeze. Breathe the air," Soona stands up and is dancing around waving his hands in the air.

"What? Where?" Graem Tan is really puzzled.

"God! God! Isn't that what you are looking for?" Soona exclaims as he spreads his hands out wide.

"Where? Where? Why can't I see Him?" Graem Tan tries to stand up and falters.

"Me! You! It! Everything! Everywhere! See! SEE!" Soona continues to dance and waves his brown hands.

"Tell Him to show Himself! Now! Please!" Graem Tan is almost pleading with tears in his eyes.

"He is showing Himself. It is showing Itself! Can't you see?" Soona kneels down and wipes away Graem Tan's tears. He helps Graem Tan to lie down, gently patting him.

"Where is He?" Graem Tan is sobbing now.

"You must understand, He is everywhere, He is everything. You cannot understand. That's why you are searching, continuously searching. Search no more. Search within. Go into yourself. He is in you, in me, in everything. Can you understand?" Soona speaks gently now.

"So I have wasted all my time. I have been blind. I have been looking everywhere except within. No wonder I can't find Him," Graem Tan continues sobbing.

"Your time is not wasted. There is no time but now. Search within. Talk to your soul. It has been waiting for you all your life. Talk to your soul. You have found God," Soona croons softly and Graem Tan closes his eyes.

"Thank you. Thank you so much. I shall get well. I am going home tomorrow. I understand now. God does not come in one form, He comes in all forms. That's why I can't find Him. I have been looking God in the eye and cannot see. Thank you for showing it to me," Graem Tan smiles at Soona.

"Yes, God is everything, God is nothing. Whatever you can see and whatever you cannot see or thought you cannot see is God. If you see this truth, you are free," Soona says soothingly and Graem Tan feels strength coming into his body.

"I am at peace now. I feel free. I haven't felt so light all my life," Graem Tan exclaims.

"The truth shall set you free. Your burden is no more. Tomorrow, you may go home," Soona flashes his famous smile, waves and skips into the jungle.

CHAPTER SIX

Corridor Of Mirrors

Maryanne is very excited. Her parents have given her permission to explore the castle. They have come to the countryside for a holiday. Her mother is arranging the food and drinks ready for a picnic. Her father and brothers are flying kites. Her younger sister is busy running after them.

But Maryanne is only interested in the castle. "I'll be back very soon," she shouts as she runs towards the castle. She looks longingly at the beautiful structure as her legs bring her nearer and nearer to it. The uphill road does not deter her. She is more exhilarated than tired. Her young, strong legs seem to be flying up the hill.

Very soon, the castle looms over her and she runs even faster. Next moment, she is before the huge entrance. The door is opened. It is welcoming her. Maryanne dances in happily. The ceiling is very high, almost three storeys high. The windows are huge and there are many of them. The hall is large but bright and beautiful.

The winding staircase is carpeted and looks so inviting. Maryanne sings delightedly as she runs up the staircase. She is soon at the first floor and she runs towards the corridor. It is the longest corridor she has ever seen! There are many mirrors hanging on both sides of the corridor. She stops at the first one. It is a gold-gilded, tastefully-designed wall mirror.

As she looks at the mirror, she sees her family members having breakfast in the dining room being reflected in the mirror. She is fascinated. This is what happened this morning. She remembers Paul, her brother, spilt some milk and was scolded by her mother. She is watching the repeat of this morning event!

She skips to the next mirror. She sees some people sitting in a horse carriage. They seem to be going on a journey. She looks closely. One of them looks like her. It is her! It is Maryanne. She wears a bonnet. She is in 19th century costume! She must be acting in a drama.

Amazed, Maryanne runs to the next mirror. It is very dark at first, then it clears and she realises that she is in a battle field. There is fighting everywhere. There are armoured men on horses and some are running around. Some are shouting while some are yelling in fright. One of them falls, the armour drops off. Maryanne screams as she sees the soldier's face. He has her face! He dies from the fatal injury.

Alarmed, she quickly runs to the next mirror. She calms down as she sees the scene of a jungle. She can hear some birds singing and the sound of the waterfall. Then, a naked figure appears and starts to swim in the river. Some moments later, more naked figures join in the swimming. One of them turns towards Maryanne and she sees her own face again!

Astounded, Maryanne runs to the next mirror. What event is she going to see this time? She sees clouds, no, they are not clouds. Is it the sky? No, it seems more like space. Yes, it is like outer space. Just like in the science fiction movies. Out of the blue, some bright lights appear. They seem to be flying in all directions. They are flickering. They are happy, Maryanne thought. One of the lights flies very close to Maryanne. She blinks as she seems to see her face smiling back at her!

Astonished, she immediately runs to the next mirror. She sees nothing. There is nothing. It is empty. She is disappointed. Suddenly, she sees many events happening in the mirror. They swirl around, many events, many people, many things, she is going dizzy. She holds her hands to her ears and screams.

Terrified, Maryanne speedily runs to the next mirror. Again, there is nothing. Afraid that the same dizzying scene may swim before her eyes, Maryanne wants to run to the next mirror. A voice stops her. "Why are you running away? Be glad, my child. What you have seen is your life. Always remember to be happy in whatever situation you find yourself. Be happy even when things seem hopeless. Especially when things seem hopeless. Be positive. SMILE and the whole world smiles with you." A face of a smiling Maryanne appears in the mirror.

Stunned, Maryanne smiles and answers, "Yes, I promise I'll always be positive, whatever happens."

"Be on your way, little one, you need not view any more mirrors, you have learnt the secret of life," the smiling Maryanne in the mirror waves at her and disappears.

CHAPTER SEVEN

Koonii And His Mistakes

Koonii has run away from home again. Yesterday, he was involved in a street fight. It was all the other boys' fault. They would not leave him alone. They always tease him about his sister, Sulii who is a cripple. Koonii cannot suppress his anger whenever anybody mentions about his sister or his family's poverty. He flies into a terrible rage and strikes at whoever is in the way.

His father does not understand his defensiveness. Koonii was beaten up by his father for ruining the family's reputation by street fighting. His father prides himself as a strict disciplinarian. They may be poor but honest and self-worthy. Even though his father regrets later that he had beaten Koonii too harshly but he supposes that Koonii needed the beating badly.

Koonii spends the night under a huge maple tree. He uses the leaves as a mattress and blanket. Fortunately, the weather is moderate as it is autumn. He does not sleep well. He tosses and turns the whole night through. Some nocturnal animals come out to peep at their new neighbour. After a while, they get tired and go back to their respective hideouts. Koonii feels lonely without his new-found friends but he is very tired and falls asleep amidst troubled thoughts.

The next morning dawns bright and clear. Koonii's street friends find him asleep under the big tree. They begin to disturb him which aroused him from his sleep. Kooni cannot contain his anger and punches out at the nearest unawared face. The startled boy falls to the ground, stunned, holding his hurting jaw. Two other boys punch Koonii repeatedly as another boy helps his injured friend to move away from the scene. After more punchings, the boys run away leaving Koonii to nurse his additional new wounds.

"Why don't they leave me alone?" Koonii asks between sobs, "What have I done to deserve this?"

He limps painfully towards a pool of water where the animals use for drinking purposes. He wets his dirty handkerchief and dabs at his wounds. The birds chirp cheerfully as Koonii sobs uncontrollably.

"What happened to you?" Koonii looks up to see the face of his neighbour, Gallii, who is old and shunned by most of the people in the neighbourhood. Normally, Koonii does not bother about Gallii either. Today, he feels so lonely, Gallii is welcomed as a friend.

"I don't understand why all these bad things always happen to me! I don't understand why everybody likes to ridicule my sister and my family. I hate them! I hate them!" Koonii shouts as he continues to nurse his wounds.

"Why do you think they like to ridicule your sister and your family?" Gallii asks.

"Because my sister is a cripple! Because my family is poor! That is why!" Koonii shouts into Gallii's face.

"Isn't it true that your sister is a cripple? Isn't it true that your family is poor? These are facts. What is there to be angry about?" Gallii asks persistently.

"But I don't like others to ridicule me because my sister is a cripple and my family is poor. I hate it!" Koonii hisses defensively.

"Why do you hate it, Koonii?" Gallii enquires calmly.

"When they ridicule my sister, I feel that something is wrong with my family. Either my parents or my sister or somebody in my family must have done something wrong. Or else my sister will not be crippled. When they said my family is poor, I feel that my father is useless or else we won't be poor. I feel that my father is not good enough. Even though I know he works very hard but still we are so poor. That is what I don't like," Koonii's voice is softening as he replies and he feels his own defensiveness weakening.

"You are defensive and unhappy because of your pride and not because of the ridicule on your sister and your family. Your sister is a cripple and your family is poor. Many of the families in the neighbourhood are poor. I am poor. It is because you cannot accept this truth that makes you so angry and rebellious," Gallii explains.

"I've never thought of it this way," Koonii looks wonderingly at Gallii. He has always looked down on this old neighbour previously. Now, he is seeing something new. Gallii does not look old or pitiful anymore.

"Now, you understand your anger, admit honestly to yourself all the reasons for flying into uncontrollable rage each time. Admit them to yourself one by one. Face the truth. Continue to admit your mistakes until they disappear totally from your mind. If you continue to dwell in the past, the past will continue to haunt you. When you face them, admit all your mistakes and you are free," Gallii says so soothingly till Koonii has forgotten his pain.

"Alright, let me try," Koonii closes his eyes and mentally counts all his mistakes. Some moments later, he heaves a sigh of relief, smiles and opens his eyes.

He finds himself sprawling all alone beside the pool of water. Gallii is gone!

CHAPTER EIGHT

Kenneth's Activities

Kenneth was caught punching one of his classmates again. His punishment was to stand outside the classroom till classes were over.

One of his classmates, Cheryl happened to walk by him on the way to the toilet. Kenneth pulled her hair as she walked pass. Cheryl screamed and Kenneth laughed. Their teacher and some of their classmates ran out from the classroom and saw Cheryl crying while Kenneth tried to pull a serious face.

"Why are you so naughty?" the teacher asked Kenneth, "You punched Ramesh just now and you bullied Cheryl now! What's wrong with you?"

Kenneth just smiled and stared at the floor.

"Naughty boys will grow into wicked men. The wicked will go to jail and when they die, they will go to hell, I want to go to hell," Kenneth looked straight into the teacher's eyes.

"What?" the teacher almost screamed.

"Hell is more interesting than heaven. They said that lots of things will happen to you in hell but if you go to heaven, you just float in the clouds and play the harp the whole day," Kenneth reflected.

"Hell is only in the mind," the teacher explained.

"But according to them, there are lots of activities in hell. I like activities not a boring life," Kenneth maintained his stand.

"Is that why you always get yourself into trouble so that you can go to hell?" the teacher looked kindly at this 10-year-old boy.

"Yes, I like to experience a lot of things. I don't like to be a goody-two shoe and have an even more boring life in heaven." Kenneth countered.

"Your life now is for you to experience as much as you want while alive on earth. You may choose any activity you like whether positive or negative. If you choose positive activities, you are already in heaven. If you choose negative activities, you are making it hell for yourself and others," the teacher told Kenneth gently.

"All right, from now on, I will try to choose positive activities. I'll try to make it more heaven than hell, teacher, I promise," Kenneth answered solemnly. "Sorry, Cheryl, I will not pull your hair again. Tell Ramesh I'm sorry I punched him. I also apologise to all the others I have bullied"

"Good, remember this, both heaven and hell are chosen by you," the teacher answered. "You don't have to do anything, you don't have to go anywhere, you don't have to be anybody, just be who you are."

CHAPTER NINE

Edward's Journey

Edward is late for work again. It has been a long night. He only staggers home at about 4.00am. He has tried explaining to Mandy repeatedly how important she is to him. He has sworn his eternal love for her, yet Mandy is set on leaving him. He has to finally give up when Paul threatens to beat him up if he pesters Mandy again. He is forced to stumble home a dejected man.

What has he done wrong? What does Paul has that he does not have? In fact, he is employed but Paul is just a hooligan, unemployed most of the time. Even whenever Paul is employed, the jobs never last more than two weeks. Moreover, Paul is constantly involved in fights. The problem is Mandy adores Paul. She says Paul is compatible with her and Paul has taste. Taste? Pah! What is taste?

"Edward!" his boss, Steven shrieks as he stands at his office door, hands upon hips, looking indignantly at Edward.

Edward stirs reluctantly from his reverie and realises that the telephone on his desk is ringing. He braces himself and picks up the telephone. Steven gives him a threatening look and disappears into his office.

It is a long day. Edward struggles to slog through the piles of paperwork making numerous mistakes in the process. He is screamed at by Steven a number of times. He finds himself running into Steven's office repeatedly and has to scurry out to amend his mistakes. His colleagues are watching him, amazed at the commotion. They are puzzled as Edward is normally an exemplary worker.

Devi, one of Edward's colleagues buys him lunch as Edward is still struggling to alter some of his glaring mistakes.

"Is something the matter? You look flustered!" Devi asks as she counts the lunch money Edward gives her.

"No, nothing, just that I woke up late and I had to hurry here and I have lost my cool," Edward smiles limply as Devi offers him a sympathetic look.

The second half of the day continues with Edward receiving more scolding and more rectifications in his work. The more he worries, the more mistakes he makes. He just cannot calm down. In fact, matters are getting worse. Isn't he glad when it is time to leave the work place. There is no more spring in his steps and certainly no happiness on his face.

Wearily, he sits down at a bench in a park, deep in thought. He is wringing his hands in despair and is sighing frenziedly. He is still evaluating over last night's occurences. What has gone wrong?

"You must be hungry. Here, have some buns," Devi's soothing voice rings in his ears.

Edward gratefully accepts the bag offered by Devi. He suddenly realises that he is famished. How long has he sat here? He smiles weakly at Devi. He has always thought her bossy, interfering and loves to meddle in other people's business. Today, he feels only gratitude for her. Nobody else realises he has missed lunch. Nobody bothers. In a crisis, you know who your friends are.

"There are ups and downs in this life," Devi sits down beside him and seems to be talking to herself but Edward can hear her. "We are here to experience the highest, the lowest and the in-between of every event. Yesterday's great is today's loser. Similarly, yesterday's goner is today's winner. Many people just have a mediocre life."

"I didn't ask to be great, I just asked for Mandy's love, I didn't ask for anything more," Edward suddenly blurts out.

"Mandy has the right to choose her love, once it was you, today it is no more," Devi insists.

"What do you know about Mandy?" Edward is defiant.

"I don't know Mandy. I just know that what is here today may be gone tomorrow," Devi continues in a soothing voice. It is a salve that rubs painfully into Edward's wound. He feels like slapping this busybody's serene face. How dare she pass such comments? And especially on Mandy, his beloved. He has forgotten that Mandy is now Paul's beloved.

"You have forgotten the reason why we are here, you cannot remember our purpose of this journey," Devi looks intently at Edward, her eyes piercing into his.

"What do you mean?" Edward is still very impatient with this nosy lady.

"You asked to come here to experience negative activities. Why are you complaining now? We were perfectly happy in Tirips Mlaer. All of us accompanied you here. See! We have multiplied and filled the earth. See! This is the purpose of this life," Devi blinks her eyes.

"Elos, oh, yes, Elos, I was Elos," Edward shields his eyes from Devi's glare.

"Yes, remember this, this is the journey you have asked for, bless every event and person that enter your life, thank them for the experience and wish them well on their chosen path, soon, you will enjoy every facet of your experience," Devi twinkles her eyes and Edward returns her smile contentedly.

CHAPTER TEN

Henry's Promise

Henry breathes in the fresh air slowly. He always stops by here on his way home. He enjoys watching the sunset as he listens to the children's laughter. As usual, he drinks in the sight of the swimmers and the surfers. Their joy and cheer tug at his heart.

He has promised his wife numerous times that he will never drink again. In fact, each time in the pub, he had made a nuisance of himself. In fact, he was the laughing stock. But then, at that time, he did not know. He thought he was the centre of attention. He thought he was popular. Everybody laughed whenever he cracked some jokes. Little did he know that they were actually laughing at him. Now, he knows. He will never allow such events to happen again.

Erica, his wife and his two children, George and Kate are always overjoyed to see him home. Henry smells dinner even before he reaches the door. There are always the same running footsteps and then, two small bodies will fling themselves at him.

"Daddy! Daddy!" two little voices echo. Four little limbs embrace him.

"Oh, my little sweeties!" Henry is overwhelmed and tears run down his cheeks.

Henry holds each one by the hand and leads them towards the dining table. Erica is always already seated at the table happily watching them. After settling George and Kate in their seats, Henry sits in his usual place.

"Oh, this is good. It smells nice. Mmm . . ," Henry puts a spoonful of food into his mouth as his wife looks on cheerfully. Both children clap their hands.

*   *   *

Henry wakes up with a start. He is sweating profusely. It always ends this way. He could almost feel the food slides down his throat. But no, it can never be. Always, this is the way it ends. He has been having the same dream every night. How he wishes he is with his family again. How he wishes he has stopped going to the pub. How he wishes he had not lost his cool.

Now, here he is. He is all alone with his dreams. At least he still has his dreams. Each night, he enjoys himself with his family again and again. This has been going on for the past ten years. In his dreams, Erica does not grow old. His children do not grow any bigger, either. Everything is the same. Exactly the same. That is his wish. Therefore, his dream.

"Your wish is my command," a voice says.

"Huh? Are you God? Are you back again?" Henry looks around frantically.

"I've been here all the while. I've never been away. Your dreams are your reality," the voice replies.

"But why does it always stop at the same place, then?" Henry retorts unbelievingly.

"Because you're not brave enough to venture further. You stop, so your dream stops," the voice continues.

"But that's the last meal I had with my family. After that, I went to the pub. I don't wish to go to the pub again. I've promised Erica not to go to the pub again," Henry protests.

"Be brave. Face your blackest moment fearlessly. Especially your blackest moment. You've been evading it for years. You've been repeating your life for years. Face it and change your life.

Confront it and your life will change. Believe me," the voice persuades.

"I'm scared. I don't want to go to the pub. I don't want to kill the man again. I don't want to be caught by the police again. I don't want to be thrown into prison again. That's why I stop the dream, each time, every time," Henry is frustrated by now.

"Conquer your fear. There is nothing to fear. It is just a dream. Treat it as a dream. Continue your journey without fear. Put in love, instead. Change the fear ingredient into love. Try it," the soothing voice continues.

"Now? Or the next time when I dream?" Henry asks sceptically.

"Whenever you are ready, I am ready," the voice offers.

Henry wrestles within himself for a long time. This voice, this God, can He be trusted? Continue the dream? Why not? What is there to lose? If he goes to the pub, he goes to the pub! He must conquer his fear! He must! He must! He must!

*   *   *

Henry breathes in the fresh air slowly. He always stops by here on his way home. He enjoys watching the sunset as he listens to the children's laughter. As usual, he drinks in the sight of the swimmers and the surfers. Their joy and cheer tug at his heart.

He has promised his wife numerous times that he will never drink again. In fact, each time in the pub, he had made a nuisance of himself. In fact, he was the laughing stock. But then, at that time, he did not know. He thought he was the centre of attention. He thought he was popular. Everybody laughed whenever he cracked some jokes. Little did he know that they were actually laughing at him. Now, he knows. He will never allow such events to happen again.

Erica, his wife and his two children, George and Kate are always overjoyed to see him home. Henry smells dinner even before he reaches the door. There are always the same running footsteps and then, two small bodies will fling themselves at him.

"Daddy! Daddy!" two little voices echo. Four little limbs embrace him.

"Oh, my little sweeties!" Henry is overwhelmed and tears run down his cheeks.

Henry holds each one by the hand and leads them towards the dining table. Erica is always already seated at the table happily watching them. After settling George and Kate in their seats, Henry sits in his usual place.

"Oh, this is good. It smells nice. Mmm . . ," Henry puts a spoonful of food into his mouth as his wife looks on cheerfully. Both the children clap their hands.

The telephone rings. Erica picks it up, speaks into it for a few minutes and her face is crestfallen. Her husband's buddies are calling him to the pub again.

"Is it Vincent? Tell him I'll meet him there," Henry announces from the table.

Erica speaks into the telephone again and hangs up. She returns to the table and continues dinner. The mood at the table has changed. The children feel it, too. Their chattering and laughter have stopped, too. Everybody just continue to eat silently. The taste and smell of the food have gone. They are just to satisfy the stomach. No more, no less.

*   *   *

The pub is crowded as usual. The moment the door swings open, you are greeted by the smoke and the revelry. It is a joyous place. Everybody is joyful. There is laughter and music all over. There is plenty of movement, too. Everybody seems to be moving. There are some still figures, hidden deep within the depths of cushions or in corners. They cannot be seen. They are not important.

Henry strolls leisurely towards his buddies, greeting all left and right like a film star. He loves the atmosphere. It is like a neighbourhood. Everybody is friendly. There are no strangers here. You may not know them. But when you wave at them, they wave back at you. This is why he loves this place. This is why he is here night after night.

Today, there is a stranger among his buddies. He has a fresh scar on his forehead. His buddies mumble a name. Henry cannot catch it because of the din. He just smiles, shakes hands and lets out some laughter as usual. Soon, he is settled and soon, starts the usual rounds of beer. Everything is as usual. Just relax, drink, joke, smile, laugh and look around.

Everything seems to be spinning. The man's face. The one with the scar. He is saying something. Henry cannot hear. He just nods his head and smiles. The man's face again. His face is twisted this time. He smashes a bottle on the table. He is holding the broken bottle. He is going to hit Henry with the bottle! Henry's buddies jump on him and are holding him down. Henry feels a surge in him. The feeling tells him to flee.

Henry finds himself running. He cannot remember anything. He continues running. He can see his house in the distance. He runs straight to the front door. He is fumbling with the key. The door suddenly opens. Erica appears from behind the door. She deftly pulls him into the house and slams the door shut.

"What happened?" Erica asks when Henry is safely in bed.

"I don't know. Everything happens so fast," Henry still feels groggy.

"Vincent called. He said a man wanted to kill you. The man said you were rude. You laughed at him. He is a tycoon's son. He dislikes insults," Erica explains.

"Is he dead?" Henry suddenly jumps up.

"No, the police took him away. Vincent said not to worry. The man's father shall take care of matters. He will be alright," Erica reassures.

"He's not dead?!" Henry is still puzzled.

"No, why should he? He wants to kill you. You could have been killed. He's fine. He could be charged. But then, Vincent said his tycoon father shall take care of everything," Erica comforts her husband.

"He's not dead. He's not dead," Henry utters over and over.

"No," Erica pats her husband's shoulder.

"Then, then . . . I'm not going to prison," Henry jumps up again.

"No, why should you? You were attacked!" Erica is surprised.

"Oh, alright, alright. I'm tired. Let me sleep," Henry surrenders.

* * *

"So you see, you can change your reality. What you thought is your reality is an illusion. You can make your illusion real. By changing your thoughts, your reality is changed. By changing your reality, everything is changed," the voice is back.

"Where am I?" Henry looks around anxiously. He heaves a sigh of relief as he sees his wife asleep beside him.

"Face your fear. Change your reality. Your reality is just an illusion. Be brave. Look fear in the eye," the voice continues.

"Yes, yes, I will. Always. I won't go to the pub anymore. It's a place where I lose all control. It has an illusion of joy and peace. I thought it has joy and peace," Henry reminisces.

"All places are the same places. The reality is within you. Change your thoughts. Your thoughts create your reality. Your illusions become real. They are your experiences. But you can change them whenever you are ready," the voice echoes in Henry's mind.

"I'm glad. I'm glad I'm home again. I promise, I promise I'll never go to the pub again, Erica," Henry mutters as he falls asleep again.

CHAPTER ELEVEN
I Am Home Again

As usual, Graeme Tan is rocking in his favourite chair under the tree. He is almost asleep when he hears light footsteps behind him. He recognises this sound. Especially the shashaying of the flapping material in the breeze.

"Dear, it's time for your medication," Mrs. Tan's voice reaches his ears.

"Thank you. I was enjoying the scenery too much. I almost fell asleep," Graeme Tan takes the tablets and the glass of water. He smiles gently at Mrs. Tan.

"Yes, things haven't changed much around here. Seems like yesterday when you came home 40 years ago. The only changes are, Jaeme is now the village doctor and Saeme is the village school teacher. They also have given us five lovely grandchildren," Mrs. Tan sighs contentedly.

"Do you blame me for vanishing on long trips so frequently during those years?" Graeme Tan looks enquiringly at his wife.

"No, not really. I understand your quest. Anyway, Jaeme and Saeme kept me very busy. I had no time to think. The only thing is, others were not so understanding," Mrs. Tan reminisces.

"Why didn't you ask me why I stopped travelling?" Graeme Tan looks wonderingly at his wife.

"I am glad you stopped. As long as you are here, I am happy," Mrs Tan answers simply.

"Yes, I was a selfish man. I am lucky to have an understanding and responsible wife like you. Can't blame others for not being understanding," Graeme Tan caresses his wife's wrinkled hands.

"It's getting dark. Let's go home before we are infested by mosquitoes," Mrs. Tan helps Graeme Tan up from the rocking chair.

* * *

The moon is exceptionally round and bright tonight. The air is very still. Everything seems to be waiting for something. Even the insects are waiting. The nocturnal animals, too.

"I must tell you about Soona. I should have told you earlier. Too many things happened after my return. I was so enthusiastic to resume my role as breadwinner after my irresponsible behaviour that I have forgotten to relate the events of my last trip," Graeme Tan whispers huskily to his sleepy wife.

"You are tired. Can't it wait until tomorrow?" Mrs. Tan asks with concern as she covers her husband's hands with the blanket.

"No, I must tell you now. I have procrastinated. Too long. Perhaps I was too tired after the last journey home. But that is no excuse," Graeme Tan tries to sit up again.

"Alright, go on. I'm listening," Mrs. Tan is apprehensive but she helps her husband to sit up.

"I found God. I found God on my last trip. So, I stopped travelling," Graeme Tan beams at his wife.

"Are you running a fever?" Mrs. Tan touches her husband's forehead.

"Listen, I am telling you the truth," Graeme Tan puts a finger on his wife's lips.

"Alright, alright. Go on," Mrs. Tan sits down resignedly.

"Do you know God? You thought you know God! I thought I didn't know God! Or I thought I know God! Or I thought I know I should know when I see God! Or I thought I would know if I see God! Or I should know if someone tells me who is God!" Graeme Tan sounds excited.

"Sh . . . Sh . . ." Mrs. Tan stands up and hushes her animated husband.

"Listen. You are not listening. I know, you think I am mad or I am going mad. I am not. You understand? Do you understand? Now, just sit down and listen," Graeme Tan grimaces at his poor wife.

"At least speak calmly. You will wake up the kids," Mrs. Tan admonishes.

"Alright, alright, I promise. Now, sit down. I will speak softly and slowly," Graeme Tan puts his fore finger to his own lips.

Mrs. Tan shakes her head as she sits down beside the bed again. She puts both her hands on her lap to show her submission.

She listens intently as Graeme Tan relates the events of his last trip. She feels herself being transported back in time to that mountain. She experiences the pain and struggle as her husband climbs. She feels like fainting as her husband lays unconscious.

She is exhilarated as her husband understands Soona's explanation. The power and the knowledge fill her body, mind and soul. Now she remembers the force of the universe. Now she feels the might of the truth. It is immeasurable. It is vast. It is limitless. It has no end. It has no beginning. It is forever and ever. And forever more. Without end.

"Dear, do you understand now?" Graeme Tan's voice is full of anxiety.

"Yes, yes, I understand now," Mrs. Tan smiles with tears flowing down her craggy cheeks.

"I have finished my tale. You were so still just now. I was afraid you were too shocked by my tale," Graeme Tan caresses his wife's crumply fingers.

"It is beautiful, so beautiful. I understand. I understand now how you felt during that trip 40 years ago. I feel everything. I experience everything. I understand now. Thank you," Mrs. Tan holds her husband's hands tight.

"I am glad. Now, I can rest," Graeme Tan slides under the blanket and prepares for sleep.

"Goodnight," Mrs. Tan kisses her husband's forehead.

"Goodnight. When you see me again, we shall be young and we shall never part. I'm going home again," Graeme Tan announces softly before he closes his eyes.

*   *   *

Mrs. Tan is supported by Jaeme and Saeme. Jaeme's wife is standing with her son and daughter on their right hand side. Saeme's husband and their three children are standing behind them. They are before the grave of Graeme Tan.

It has been two years since Graeme Tan passed away that fateful night. Mrs. Tan will always remember that night. That was the most unusual night. Tonight, she must tell her children what happened that night. She has procrastinated, too.

CHAPTER TWELVE
Koonii's Sacrifice

Koonii lays hunched in his rickety bed. He has not moved for hours. But his mind is racing. There are many questions plaguing him. Too many. Why? Why? Why is his family so poor? Why is he not good looking? Why is his sister, Sulii a cripple? Gallii has assisted in helping him forgive and forget. The problem is, the moment he steps into the classroom, the jeering and snide remarks begin.

Then, his anger mounts again and again. He has tried controlling his temper. He has not gotten into any fight since the talk with Gallii. But others are still talking non-stop about him and his family. Every angle he turns, he can see the smirk on their faces. He has tried wiping out every image from his mind. He has tried concentrating on his studies. But he can still hear the laughter. And the way they shy away whenever he comes near.

He does not know how much longer he can take it. In fact, he wants sorely to slap every one of those simpering faces. Instead, he has meditated as encouraged by Gallii. The more he meditates, the more they poke fun at him. They are relentless. Why? Why? Why me?

He stiffens as he hears the door creaks open. The light sunshine creeps in for a while and vanishes just as quickly as the door closes. Alternating light and heavy footsteps indicates his sister, Sulii.

"Here, you must be hungry," Koonii looks up to see Sulii holding out a bowl of porridge towards him.

"Thanks, you need not bring me my lunch. I should have taken it for myself," Koonii indicates his sister's problem leg.

"It's already past lunch time. I've reheated the porridge for you. I thought you must be very busy with your school work. So I bring your lunch for you," the bed creaks as Sulii sits on it.

"I was just thinking about something. I didn't realise it's past lunch time. I'm sorry to make you worry," Koonii looks embarrassed.

"What are you thinking about? Perhaps I can help," Sulii offers as her hands reach for Koonii's school books.

"It's not those. It's something else. Never mind, I'll solve it myself," Koonii gulps down some porridge hurriedly.

"I know, since you stop fighting with the neighbourhood boys, your studies have improved. Father is very pleased," Sulii beams at her brother.

"But they are still taunting me!" Koonii suddenly blurts out. He regrets it but it is too late.

"You mean, those boys?" Sulii looks kindly at him.

"No, everyone, all of them. I fought with the boys. But the girls too made fun of us. I want to slap them all," Koonii shows his tight fist.

"What's there for them to gossip about?" Sulii asks wonderingly.

"Lots. We are poor. You are crippled. I am not good looking. Mother is old and wrinkled. Father is not smart. Our house is dilapidated. That's why I study hard. At least, I am smarter than most of them," Koonii's eyes flash with anger.

"Most of the families in the neighbourhood are poor. Most of their parents are old, too. I don't see any difference between us and them," Sulii tries to comfort her brother.

"But they don't have a crippled sister!" Koonii almost spits at his sister.

"There is no guilt in being poor, old, ugly or crippled, Koonii. There is only guilt in thinking that being poor, old, ugly or crippled is blameworthy. It is not easy to be poor, old, ugly or crippled," Sulii replies soothingly.

Koonii looks at Sulii with shock. He suddenly seems to hear Gallii's voice. This is not Sulii speaking. It is Gallii! Sulii does not have the intelligence to speak thus!

"Are you Sulii?" Koonii looks suspiciously at his sister.

"Yes, I'm Sulii. Don't I look like Sulii?" his sister gives him an astonished look.

"But . . . but you sounded like somebody else. You don't normally speak like this," Koonii is mumbling confusedly.

"I'm Sulii and I'm talking to you. I've been watching you. I know there is much turmoil in you. You must understand this. If not, you will constantly be struggling within yourself. Relax and listen to me," Sulii offers.

"It is a sacrifice to be poor, old, ugly or crippled. These are the ones who have sacrificed the most. Do not look at such beings with pity or disdain. Look on them with gratitude and blessings. Wish them well. Somebody has to take up such bodies. If not them, then you," Sulii admonishes wisely.

"It must be difficult for you to be crippled. I never think of it this way. I am always angry. At least, I am not crippled," Koonii brushes away his tears.

"I'm used to it. I've accepted it since I knew this is what I have to live with. Happiness is to accept everything including all the negative remarks by others. Wish them well for they are ignorant. Bless them for they will understand sooner or later. One day, they will thank you for your sacrifice," Sulii predicts.

"I know. I understand now. I'll accept all these as you have accepted them. No wonder you are always so cheerful and happy. I have always wondered why. Thanks for sharing your thoughts," Koonii slurps the remains from the bowl.

CHAPTER THIRTEEN

The Enemy Is Us

Scenario: During World War Two

<u>In the camp of Batallion Six</u>

Sergeant: Get ready, guys! We are moving in tonight! We must move before the enemy is ready! Check your equipment. Hausen, get ready to sneak near the enemy camp and report the situation to me immediately!

Hausen: Yes, sir!

Hausen runs towards the direction of the enemy camp. The other soldiers move quickly to pack their gear and check their ammunition, helping each other to load their backpack. Every move is carried out in perfect order.

Near the enemy camp

Hausen can see fire light before he sees any other movement. He knows he is approaching the enemy camp. He can see their flag flapping in the night breeze. It is the enemy's flag. He moves silently and hides behind the thick tree trunks as he slithers along like a snake.

He is now 100 metres from the enemy camp. He sees two sentries near to where he is. He scans the area for other sentries. He sees another two walking on his left hand side and another two on his right side. The enemy is prepared and they are very careful. Bad news!

Suddenly, a soldier of authority approaches and both the sentries on his left saluted silently. Hausen puts on his binoculars to focus on the soldiers' faces. He lets out a sharp breath!

After calming himself, Hausen slithers backwards till he is in the thick of the jungle again. Then he stands and runs, and runs, and runs back to his camp. He is running so fast that he almost collapses.

In the camp of Batallion Six Again

Sergeant: Good, bring Hausen in when he is rested!

Hausen enters with a pale face and gasping breath.

Hausen: Sergeant, Sergeant, the enemy is us, the enemy is us!!

Sergeant: Shut up, man! Are you crazy, man!? Tell me, what did you see?!

Hausen: The enemy! The enemy! They are us! I saw you and I saw everybody over there! They are us! Stop! Stop! We must not kill ourselves! We are they and they are us!

Sergeant: Send him away! Fool! Derrick, go and check out the enemy! Now!

Derrick runs towards the direction of the enemy camp.

Near the enemy camp

After a while, Derrick can see the fire light before he sees any other movement. He knows he is approaching the enemy camp. He can see their flag flapping in the night breeze. It is the enemy's flag. He moves silently and hides behind the thick tree trunks as he slithers along like a snake.

He is now 100 metres from the enemy camp. He sees two sentries near to where he is. He scans the area for other sentries. He sees another two walking on his left hand side and another two on his right side. The enemy is prepared and they are very careful. Bad news!

Suddenly, a soldier of authority approaches and both the sentries on his left saluted silently. Derrick puts on his binoculars to focus on the soldiers' faces. He lets out a sharp breath!

After calming himself, Derrick slithers backwards till he is in the thick of the jungle again. Then he stands and runs, and runs, and runs back to his camp. He is running so fast that he almost collapses.

<u>In the camp of Batallion Six Again</u>

Sergeant: Good, bring Derrick in when he is rested!

Derrick enters with a pale face and gasping breath.

Derrick: Sergeant, Sergeant, the enemy is us, the enemy is us!!

Sergeant: Shut up, man! Are you crazy, man!? Tell me, what did you see?!

Derrick: The enemy! The enemy! They are us! I saw you and I saw everybody over there! They are us! Stop! Stop! We must not kill ourselves! We are they and they are us!

Sergeant: Send him away! Fool! Ivan, go and check out the enemy! Now!

Ivan runs towards the direction of the enemy camp.

Near the enemy camp

After a while, Ivan can see the fire light before he sees any other movement. He knows he is approaching the enemy camp. He can see their flag flapping in the night breeze. It is the enemy's flag. He moves silently and hides behind the thick tree trunks as he slithers along like a snake.

He is now 100 metres from the enemy camp. He sees two sentries near to where he is. He scans the area for other sentries. He sees another two walking on his left hand side and another two on his right side. The enemy is prepared and they are very careful. Bad news!

Suddenly, a soldier of authority approaches and both the sentries on his left saluted silently. Ivan puts on his binoculars to focus on the soldiers' faces. He lets out a sharp breath!

After calming himself, Ivan slithers backwards till he is in the thick of the jungle again. Then he stands and runs, and runs, and runs back to his camp. He is running so fast that he almost collapses.

In the camp of Batallion Six Again

Sergeant: Good, bring Ivan in when he is rested!

Ivan enters with a pale face and gasping breath.

Ivan: Sergeant, Sergeant, the enemy is us, the enemy is us!!

Sergeant: Shut up, man! Are you crazy, man!? Tell me, what did you see?!

Ivan: The enemy! The enemy! They are us! I saw you and I saw everybody over there! They are us! Stop! Stop! We must not kill ourselves! We are they and they are us!

Sergeant: Send him away! Fools! How many fools do I have in my camp?!

The sergeant runs towards the direction of the enemy camp.

Near the enemy camp

After a while, the sergeant can see the fire light before he sees any other movement. He knows he is approaching the enemy camp. He can see their flag flapping in the night breeze. It is the enemy's flag. He moves silently and hides behind the thick tree trunks as he slithers along like a snake.

He is now 100 metres from the enemy camp. He sees two sentries near to where he is. He scans the area for other sentries. He sees another two walking on his left hand side and another two on his right side. The enemy is prepared and they are very careful. Bad news!

Suddenly, a soldier of authority approaches and both the sentries on his left saluted silently. The sergeant puts on his binoculars to focus on the soldiers' faces. He lets out a sharp breath!

After calming himself, the sergeant slithers backwards till he is in the thick of the jungle again. Then he stands and runs, and runs, and runs back to his camp. He is running so fast that he almost collapses.

In the camp of Batallion Six Again

The sergeant's face is very pale and he is gasping for breath.

Sergeant: The enemy is us, the enemy is us!! The enemy! The enemy! They are us! I saw me and I saw everybody over there! They are us! Stop! Stop! We must not kill ourselves! We are they and they are us!

CHAPTER FOURTEEN

The Mirror

The shouting is still going on outside. Maryanne and her sister, Joanne are huddled in bed. They are hidden under the thick blanket and they have stuffed their pillows against their ears. This does not snuff out the commotion, nevertheless. Worst, sounds of smashing plates against walls and floors started. It is going to be a long day.

Since Maryanne's mother found out about Aunty Claire, all hell has broken loose. The once tranquil house is no more. There were shouting matches as soon as her father steps into the house. There were occasions when her father did not come home for days and weeks.

The problem is, the moment he appears, the shouting starts, almost always ending with throwing of things and the quick exit of her father. Maryanne and her sister had a hard time helping their mother to clean up after each fight.

Today, however, something different is happening outside. The shouting has been going on and on for far too long. What is the matter? Her father should have been gone long ago. But, no, the fighting continues. Joanne starts crying and Maryanne tries to comfort her.

Suddenly, their room door opens. Both the girls stiffen and hold their breath. The footsteps indicate that it is their mother. Both girls heave a sigh of relief. They emerge from the blanket and sit up in bed as their mother sits down heavily. Her face is drawn and she has aged a lot these past few weeks. Maryanne feels deep sadness in her heart.

"I am going to grandma's house for a few days. You two be good while I'm away. Father is bringing Aunty Claire over after dinner. Now, you two be good and go help clear up downstairs," Connie said wearily as drops of tears flow down her cheek.

"Yes, mom," both girls answer dutifully and creep downstairs.

*　　*　　*

And so, mother shifts out and Aunty Claire shifts in. The shouting is no more. The girls are glad about this. But things are not the same anymore. Mother and Aunty Claire are not the same. Oh, yes, Aunty Claire is very kind and even coaches them after school. But it is just not the same. Mother is mother, Aunty Claire is Aunty Claire.

*   *   *

It is a fine sunny day. It rained last night which makes it an even better day. The air is cool and the wind is cool. Maryanne, Joanne and Aunty Claire are sitting in the garden sipping lemonade and eating cakes. Aunty Claire is a good cook, better than mother. There is a twinge in Maryanne's heart. How can she be so unfaithful to mother? The dark thought vanishes immediately when Aunty Claire touches her cheek. Maryanne smiles gratefully at Aunty Claire.

At that moment, father comes home. He is holding a bunch of flowers and he is smiling. Father is always smiling these days. Maryanne does not remember her father smiling even before the fights with mother. The only happy time they had was when they visited the old castle long ago. Yes, long ago. It seems like another life time. Maryanne suddenly realises that their parents' relationship had started deteriorating long ago.

She had been blind. Why hadn't she noticed it before? Maybe because her parents kept it from them. Especially the boys. Now, the boys are in college. They have not seen Aunty Claire yet. In fact, nobody has informed them about the abrupt change in their lives. Now, what is father saying? No, it must be a mistake. No, Joanne is smiling and Aunty Claire is kissing both her cheeks. There is even a twinkle in father's eyes.

"Yes, from now on, Aunty Claire is mom," father repeats and smiles fondly at the three of them.

"Mom?" Maryanne is confused.

"Yes," Aunty Claire kisses Maryanne's cheeks as well.

"No, no," Maryanne brushes away Aunty Claire's face and runs into the house.

*　　*　　*

As usual, Maryanne buries herself in her thick blanket and cries her heart out. She cries and cries till she cannot cry anymore. Lying there in deep remorse, she hears someone calling her.

"Go away," Maryanne hissed.

"Maryanne!" the voice is louder this time. Maryanne looks up. It is not father's voice. It is not Joanne's voice. And it is not Aunty Claire's voice, either. And the voice is from inside the room. But she has locked the door. She throws back the blanket and looks around wildly.

"Who are you? Where are you?" Maryanne looks at the opened window, the curtains flapping in the wind.

"Here, come here," the voice comes from the mirror. An image is forming.

Maryanne climbs out of bed hurriedly and rushes towards the mirror. She sees herself, no, not herself but an adult Maryanne.

"It's you, what do you want?" Maryanne suddenly remembers the corridor of mirrors in the castle. She sits down before her vanity table.

"You promised to be positive, do you remember?" adult Maryanne asks smilingly.

"But mom is gone. Now Aunty Claire becomes mom. That means mom will not come back," Maryanne mutters miserably.

"Are you happy with Aunty Claire?" the mirror asks again.

"Yes, I love Aunty Claire. Father is happy. Joanne loves her, too. But she is not mom," Maryanne's confusion returns.

"See, I am mom. See, I am Aunty Claire. See, I am Maryanne," the images in the mirror changes and rotates and changes and rotates non-stop.

"Can you see? Can you see?" the mirror keeps urging as Maryanne stares. She closes her eyes as she feels dizzy.

"What is this? What is the meaning of this?" Maryanne opens her eyes and the images are still changing and rotating.

"I am mom. I am Aunty Claire. I am Maryanne. We are the same, be positive" the images stop at Aunty Claire. Aunty Claire smiles lovingly at her.

"Be positive," Maryanne repeats and assures herself and looks at Aunty Claire but now mom is there.

"Be happy, we are the same, always and forever," adult Maryanne appears and waves at her. The images disappear and she sees herself in the mirror.

She looks deep into the mirror, then she smiles and waves back. Yes, she understands now. Mom is Aunty Claire. Aunty Claire is mom. Forever and ever. She runs out of her room happily and looks for Aunty Claire.

CHAPTER FIFTEEN
Ye Are A Part Of Me

It is drizzling. You can hear the wind singing as the gentle breeze caresses you, envelopes you and leaves you, then returns and caresses you, envelopes you and leaves you again and again and again. As the raindrops increase, the wind blows harder and a piece of the mountain falls off.

The mountain has been the shadow to many hills, rivers and valleys. It has been the home to many trees, plants and foliage. It has been the shelter to many animals, humans and birds. It is also the shield to many sand, stones, rocks and earth.

Now, this piece of the mountain falls off. It has left its source. As it falls, it breaks into many smaller pieces. Some become bigger rocks. Some become smaller rocks. Some become pebbles. Some become bigger stones. Some become smaller stones. Some become sand. This piece of the mountain has separated into many parts.

Some of the bigger rocks become smaller shelters to humans, animals and birds like the mountain. They are very happy. "See, even though we have fallen from the mountain, we are still useful." These bigger rocks rejoice.

However, some of the bigger rocks kill some animals, humans and birds upon impact of the fall. They are very depressed. "I don't mean to take any lives. It is just an accident. I am so sorry." Later, they also become shelters to humans, animals and birds but these bigger rocks live with regret for the rest of their lives.

Some of the smaller rocks become roads, walkways and drains. They are very contented. "See, even though we have fallen from the mountain, we are still useful." These smaller rocks are thankful.

Meanwhile, some of the smaller rocks fall on some animals, humans and birds and injure them. They feel very sorrowful. "Oh, oh, I don't mean to hurt you. Oh, oh, I am so sorry you have to be in pain because of me. Oh, do forgive me." These smaller rocks continue to moan till the minor wounds of the animals, humans and birds are healed. They feel better when they become roads, walkways and drains but they cannot forgive themselves for the permanent injuries inflicted on the animals, humans and birds.

Some of the pebbles are picked up by humans to be used for decoration and healing purposes. They feel very grateful. "See, even though we have fallen from the mountain, we are still useful." These pebbles sing happily.

Still, other pebbles fall into the river. Some fishes are injured while some are killed. These pebbles are grief-stricken. They moan long and loud for the dead fishes. They moan even longer for the injured fishes as these fishes never recovered and died after suffering for a long period of time. Some of the injured fishes are eaten by other fishes. Nonetheless, these pebbles stop moaning when they are gathered by humans to be used for decoration and healing purposes. But they cannot forget the fishes they have injured and lives that they have taken.

Some of the smaller stones are used by humans for building purposes. They are exultant. "See, even though we have fallen from the mountain, we are still useful." These stones are jubilant.

Conversely, some smaller stones hurt some animals, humans and birds during the fall. They are despondent. "It is not our intention. We don't mean to hurt you. Oh, we are so sorry." These stones plead till they are gathered by humans for useful purposes.

Some of the sand is gathered by humans for building purposes. They are hilarious. "See, even though we have fallen from the mountain, we are still useful." These stones are triumphant.

On the other hand, some of the sand fall upon humans, animals and birds and blinded them. They are remorseful. They cry till they are gathered by humans for useful purposes. However, they are still sad over their carelessness.

"Oh, don't cry, my children," the mountain comforts them, "do not feel regret. The past is over. This is the most important moment. Be happy and useful every present moment. If you always rejoice now, this present moment is a gift from me. It is my present to you."

"You were a part of me and you will again be a part of me. In fact, you are never apart from me. I will always be with you and you will return to me someday," the mountain reassures them.

"Yes, yes, we shall be happy and useful till we reunite with you again," all the parts of the mountain answer joyfully.

CHAPTER SIXTEEN
The Culmination

Ben watches with satisfaction as the vegetable leaves sway in the breeze. He enjoys standing at the hilltop to watch the changing landscape as the sun sets. Every sunset is different. He has them all in his memory. Yet all is the same. It is the same sun and the same sky. Yet all is different.

He will always remember his dream and his mother's dream years ago. That time in the sea of flowers. He will never forget. That's why now he is a farmer. He produces food for the people in the neighbourhood. These people he knows are also himself. He will never forget the dream. He will perpetuate the dream.

*   *   *

Kenneth collapses onto the wooden bunk in the hut. He is dead tired. But he has to carry on. He loves activities. He has been a philanthropist for years. After his college days, he has volunteered his services in poverty stricken countries. Especially the underdeveloped and undeveloped areas. He is always happy to see the results of his work.

Today has been a long day. Since dawn till noon, he has been teaching a group of children. Thereafter, he has been helping the medical team. Before retiring for the day, he was mending the fishing boats and nets. Tomorrow, he has promised to help in the farming work.

He has many busy self-satisfying days. He never idles. He has created heaven on earth. He has fulfilled his dreams. Daily, he thanks his teacher silently for showing him the way.

* * *

Henry sighs happily as the gush of wind seems to bring in the tide. He is happy he can stand here again. He absorbs the children's voices and their laughter into his bloodstream. He is grateful he can walk on this beach again and again and again. He can feel the sand slides away at his every step. They are a part of him.

He saunters leisurely as he breathes in every minute, tasting the sweet air. He smiles joyfully at the expectation of Erica and his kids waiting for him eagerly at home. He quickens his footsteps at these thoughts. Now, he really appreciates his family life. He will always appreciate them. He remembers how he has created his reality. Always. And always.

*   *   *

The sergeant waves the flag as he finishes his story. "Peace! Peace! We are they and they are us! Peace! Peace!" This is always the conclusion of all his talks. Everybody claps as they salute the respected old sergeant. He is constantly surrounded by his soldiers of old, Hausen, Derrick, Ivan and all the rest in Battalion Six.

They have been his staunch supporters all these years. They have been proclaiming peace and organising peace talks with many heads of states and organisations. They have been sharing their beliefs far and wide. The events they saw that night near the enemy camp. They will never forget. Never.

The sergeant and the battalion have concluded that everybody is one and the same. This is the message they are proclaiming. What joy and happiness they have now. This is the true joy from their hearts. This is the eternal message.

*   *   *

You can always smell the roses. The perfume permeated the whole house. Only the aroma of the baking from the kitchen can compete with it. There are sounds of joy and laughter in the garden. There are shrieks and running footsteps in the back yard, too. There is no end to the number of occupants in this house.

Mrs. Saw moves around with a walking stick attempting to follow her grandchildren. They have been visiting her every weekend. She remembers all their names. But she has to keep up with them as years go by. They grow so fast. And they can move around so fast. But she is happy with the joyous atmosphere now.

Since Miss Cornelia's visit, things have changed. Mrs. Saw at last understands that happiness is within. She has never force her children and grandchildren to drop by. Miraculously, they appear every weekend. Now, Mrs. Saw sees the joy.

* * *

Devi is dancing happily as her skirt twirls and flaps in the air. All the children are clapping as they dance around Devi. They love dancing classes. This is the time when they can express themselves with their body movements. Devi loves teaching the children, too.

Edward smiles lazily as he scrutinises the art papers. He enjoys watching Devi dancing with the children. All these movements, so graceful and full of happiness. The children's laughter fills his days and nights. Their joyful expressions remain even during his painting classes. He enjoys teaching them, too.

Since the talk he had with Devi long, long ago, both of them have decided to assist as many children as possible to lead happy lives. This they do by offering dancing and painting classes at many orphanages and nursery schools.

Now, they share a deep sense of fulfilment. Now is the moment to fill the children's hearts with love and joy. Love and joy fill their hearts, too. It will go on forever and ever.

* * *

Aunty Claire looks lovely, today. It is her seventieth birthday. It has been a long time since she wore a beautiful gown. She has been sick and bed ridden for years. Maryanne and Joanne are fussing over her. Their brothers, Tim and David are attending to the guests. Their father has passed away some years back.

Maryanne has always respected Aunty Claire while Joanne has accepted Aunty Claire right from the beginning. Years have pass, her siblings have married and have their own families except Maryanne. She has made it her duty to stay with Aunty Claire. She knows that love for Aunty Claire is love for her mother.

Love is all there is. There is nothing else. Whether Aunty Claire or mother, all is the same. Maryanne has remained positive since the talk with the mirror. Thank you mirror.

* * *

Koonii looks at the bright shining eyes of the group of students. They are listening intently as Koonii explains a concept to them. He loves teaching them. He knows how to teach concepts interestingly to command their attention. He uses models and examples which appeal to these students. Most of them will be dreaming as he teaches. Koonii does not mind. He loves creativity. He prefers this way of teaching.

From their dreamy expressions, Koonii knows his students are absorbing his concepts. When the classes end, most of them are reluctant to leave. They have lots of questions. Their curiosity stirs Koonii's heart. He understands their quest. He is just as curious as he was years ago.

He remembers his two teachers, Gallii and Sulii. They are the best teachers he ever has. He will always remember what they taught him. He is sharing their teachings with others. He is helping others to understand as he had understood many years ago.

* * *

Jaeme and Saeme are in tears as Mrs. Tan relates her tale. They experience the struggle as their father, Graeme Tan climbs the mountain. They feel the exhilaration as the understanding fills their hearts. The love and joy are immeasurable. Nothing can compare with these.

They are like birds flying in the sky. Free and soaring in the sky. No, more like the universe. They can feel the moon, stars, sun and the eternal space. The eternity of space is welcomed. This is the peace that is awaiting them. Mrs. Tan is soaring with her children. When they return to earth, Mrs. Tan encourages them to relate the same to their children and to their children's children. Forever and ever.

*   *   *

The bigger rocks have disintegrated and melded with the earth. They have served their purpose. The smaller rocks have also melded much earlier. They have performed their task. The pebbles have mixed with the cobbled path. The job is done. The smaller stones have united with the earth. They have completed their experiences. The sand and the earth cannot be separated. They have become one.

Yes, we are one, the bigger rocks, the smaller rocks, the pebbles, the smaller stones and the sand declare. We are one, always and forever. We are reunited with the mountain, our source. We shall never part. We are now a part of the mountain, our source.

Yes, dear ones, we are one again, acquiesced the mountain. We have always been one. We are never apart. We are always a part of each other. Now, at last, you can see. We shall always be together.

CHAPTER SEVENTEEN
The Eternal Moment

B en feels himself expanding. He is floating, flying, surging. He feels very light, weightless. He feels love. He feels his mother's feathery touch. Exactly like the days when he was hurt and how his mother used to sooth him. He feels his father's hug.

He is surrounded by all his family, his friends and many strangers. All of them exude love. Love and nothing else. He feels blissfully happy. Exulted. He is shouting with bliss but no sound can be heard. His shouting echoes within. It is a song of silence.

He gives himself up to this cloak of intense feeling. He abandons himself to it for he is satisfied. As he surrenders, he feels himself being merged with his family, friends and many strangers. Just like the many Bennies that he saw, they are him. They are united.

* * *

Kenneth feels very light, extraordinarily light. He is like a feather. He allows himself to float freely. It is so refreshing after carrying his aching bones for so long. He had a very active life. But it has taken a toll on his physical body. He welcomes a rest.

He blithely greets this lightness. He rejoices in the release. He feels others surrounding him, his parents, his siblings, his classmates, his friends, his teachers, his relatives and many other strangers. He is engulfed by them. He sings with joy as their love touches his heart.

They converge and become one. Together they soar higher and higher, freer and freer.

* * *

Henry is ecstatic. He is turning round and round. He seems to be in a whirlpool. The difference is there are many others silhouetting with him. He is mildly surprised that among them are his old friends from the pub, including the man with the scar, his family members, his many long lost friends and other strangers. He feels only happiness. He smiles. Erica and his children are in his arms again.

They are revolving faster and faster. Henry feels almost dizzy from the revolutions as well as by the overwhelming love emanated from within. He feels very light as he abandons himself to the spinning force.

He laughs as he is enfolded within the rotating body. As a single body, they continue to gyrate and become lighter and lighter.

*   *   *

The sergeant clasps his soldiers of old, Hausen, Derrick, Ivan and all the rest in Battalion Six. He is magnanimous. In his bosom are also the other battalions and the enemy battalions. He guffaws with happiness as the rest is incorporated within his embrace.

He grows bigger and bigger. More and more are sucked into his bosom. The listeners, the audience in his talks and seminar. The whole world. Everybody. He chuckles with delight. There are echoes of his laughter, their laughter. They resounded in every direction. There is love and happiness all over.

They continue to inflate, adding on more and more figures. There is no end. Not yet.

*   *   *

Mrs. Saw moves towards the illumination. No, she is the light. She is dazzling. She is a shining star. Her light shines upon hundreds, thousands, millions, billions. She is amazed. Understanding dawn upon her as she sees her parents, her siblings, her husband, her children, her grandchildren, her friends, her neighbours and most of all Miss Cornelia. Yes, Miss Cornelia.

Yes, this is the eternal joy. Joy emanated from within. Her joy is the light that illuminated everything and everyone. They are shining as well. They have also become sparkling, twinkling stars. Yes, all is bathed in perfect light.

They shine together as one. They have become one star and one light.

*   *   *

Edward finds himself speeding in a vast vacuum. He spreads his arms and feels the coolness of the space. He feels free. He has never been free, even in Tirips Mlaer. But now, he is free. He hits at nothing with his fist. At once, he is surrounded by many others. He sees his parents, his friends, his colleagues, his students and many other strangers. Yes, his boss, Stephen and Devi are here, too. And yes, all from Tirips Mlaer, too.

Oh, it feels so good to be encircled by so many others. He stretches out his arms and embraces them. They bond together and become a huge Edward or is it a huge Stephen or a huge Devi? He is not sure. It does not matter. They have become one body.

Together, as one body, they continue speeding through the void.

*   *   *

Maryanne feels her body flattening. She is paper thin, no, even thinner. At the same time, she is emanating brightness. She is shimmering. Oh, she is the mirror. No, she is in the mirror. She swirls around. Oh, yes, there is Aunty Claire and mother. They are holding hands, smiling at her simultaneously. Maryanne moves towards them.

As Maryanne moves nearer, more figures appear. Her father, grandparents, brothers and sisters, her friends, her relatives and many strangers appear. They move towards her as well. They continue to move forwards. They merge into one.

Together they rise and expand, mirror, castle and all.

*   *   *

Koonii sees many figures rushing around. They are moving rapidly. He can hardly see them. They are subtle beings. He wishes to join them. Whoosh! He feels himself entangled with the rushing bodies. He is part of them. Now he knows. He must relax. As he does so, he is enlightened.

He feels the presence of his parents, his sister, dear Sulii and his teacher, Gallii, his neighbours, his classmates, his students and so many other strangers. All of them are wrapped within the rushing force. He can feel the fondness that Sulii has for him.

He feels Gallii's kindness. He feels the love from his parents, his neighbours, his classmates and his students. He feels the love from the countless strangers encircling him.

He abandons himself. He is merging with the force, gathering more force. They are united and continue their swishing around as an ever increasing force.

* * *

Graeme Tan is vibrating fast. He is vibrating faster and faster. He is oscillating. As he vibrates, he feels other forces joining him. They enfold him. He is being swallowed whole by the force. He sees Soona, his wife, Mrs. Tan, his children, Jaeme and Saeme, his grandchildren, his friends, his acquaintances and other strangers within the fold.

They are vibrating rapidly. They are gaining momentum as more and more bodies join them. They are growing, bloating like an inflated balloon. But Graeme Tan can feel only happiness and love within the enlarging body. The more they vibrate, the more love he feels. He surrenders himself to it totally.

He is contented and satisfied. At last, he sees and he knows the truth.

* * *

The bigger rocks, the smaller rocks, the pebbles, the smaller stones and the sand are ascending to reunite with the mountain. The earth is rotating fast to merge with the moon, sun, stars and other planets. All the solar systems and galaxies are amalgamated. There is no separation between them.

Ben, Kenneth, Henry, the sergeant, Mrs. Saw, Edward, Maryanne, Kooni, Graeme Tan and their enlarging bodies have integrated with the amalgamated solar systems and galaxies. They have reunited at last. All is vibrating fast.

The expansion stops. All is constricting, constricting, constricting. The space is being shut out. All is becoming matter. All that has been separated has combined as one. It has diminished into a small dot. A solid matter. A tiny dot. A minute dot. The dot has almost vanished. There is no more matter. Only energy exists. Nothing matters.

All is still. Serene. For a moment. Just a moment. In a flash, the dot burst forth again! Space came to be. Matter expands. Forms of various shapes and sizes come into being. The cycle begins again. Ben, Kenneth, Henry, the sergeant, the soldiers, Mrs. Saw, Edward, Maryanne, Koonii, Graeme Tan, our families, our friends, our neighbours, our enemies, strangers, their enlarging bodies and the amalgamated solar systems and galaxies are once more separated again. It is a circle. Going on and on. World without end.

CHAPTER EIGHTEEN
All Is One

At first, nothing is
Then, everything is
The cosmos, the galaxies
All oceans, all seas

Many beings come to be
Some with eyes that cannot see
Serene are the wise
The rest on the rise

Experiences are why we are here
Even down, continue your cheer
All is temporary
Look towards our sanctuary

The promise is real
We need not fear
Love is the all
None will fall

All will share
Do not despair
Strong as the sun
All is one.

Elos, do you remember now?

Bless all who give you the experiences. You ask for it. You want interesting, exciting times, remember? Tirips Mlaer was perfect but boring, remember?

We come from Tirips Mlaer! All of us! God has sent us nothing but ANGELS.

REMEMBER, always, REMEMBER!

Anyway, continue to enjoy your life as it is. It is your choice, whether King or beggar.

Be happy!

(Tirips Mlaer) Spirit Realm spelt backwards, SEE?? Because we have left it. When we return to it, it will be Spirit Realm.

THERE IS HOPE FOR EVERYBODY!! REJOICE!!